WINNING
IN YOUR
FINANCE$

How to Walk God's Pathway to Prosperity

Winning In Your Finances:
How to Walk God's Pathway
to Prosperity

Published by Mac Hammond Ministries, a.k.a.,
Living Word Christian Center
© 2003 Living Word Christian Center
ISBN: 1-57399-168-6

Mac Hammond Ministries
P.O. Box 29469
Minneapolis, MN 55429-2946

WINNING IN YOUR FINANCES:
How to Walk God's Pathway to Prosperity

Poverty equals godliness. It's a mindset deeply entrenched in the thinking of literally millions of Christians. Religion and tradition have conditioned them to believe that it's not only useless to ask God to prosper you, it is actually sinful.

That's why "the prosperity message," as it has come to be called, has generated so much controversy in recent years. The idea that God may actually want you to increase financially runs counter to nearly everything many of us have been taught. A few people get downright offended if you dare to suggest God would have them be anything but poor and miserable this side of heaven!

The liberating truth is that God's will for His children is increase, sufficiency, and abundance in every area of their lives. His Word clearly tells us so; it lays out many different principles about prosperity that are vital to understand. I don't have time in this book to explain each of these principles, but I would like to lay a foundation upon which you can begin to walk the Winner's Way in the financial arena.

Chapter 1

GOD WANTS YOU PROSPEROUS!

There are few qualities more critical to ongoing success than proper perspective. Viewing the circumstances and situations of life through the right "lens" is at the heart of godly wisdom. This is especially true in the financial arena, for the Bible clearly states the "love" of money (not money itself) is the root of all evil. (1 Timothy 6:10)

To properly navigate and win God's way in the financial arena, we must have a proper perspective toward it. With that in mind, I want to share with you three important "lenses" you must look through before you can begin to walk God's pathway to prosperity.

The first thing that must be clear in your mind is that God does want you to prosper and is not against you having things. A wealth of Scripture clearly proves this fact while also showing us He is against "things having you!" Things (money) have you when they occupy the place God is to hold in your life and you "forget" God by placing your "trust" in riches. (1 Timothy 6:17, Deut. 8:10-11)

Thus the issue is our perspective toward money and how we use it—not does God want us to prosper. There is only one reliable way to be assured of this truth: go to His Word. There is no shortage of Scriptures that speak directly to this issue. Although space does not permit us to look at all of them here, a sampling will give us a clear picture of God's intentions.

In Deuteronomy 8:18, God makes a remarkable statement:

> *But thou shalt remember the Lord thy*
> *God: for it is he that giveth thee power*
> *to get wealth, that he may establish his*
> *covenant which he sware unto thy*
> *fathers, as it is this day.*

Ask yourself a question. Why would God tell His covenant people He was giving them the power to get wealth if He didn't want them to have any? *But Mac, that verse isn't for us, it was written to the Old Testament Jews!* you may be thinking.

Many believers rob themselves of hundreds of wonderful Bible promises through such an assumption. They think that because the promises were originally made to Israel (the children of Abraham) in the Old Testament, they don't apply to them as well.

The New Testament says we have a better covenant established on better promises.

> *But now He [Jesus] has obtained a more excellent ministry, inasmuch as He is also mediator of a better covenant established on better promises.*
> (Hebrews 8:6)

Also, if you are a child of God, those blessings of Abraham are yours to claim:

> *That the blessing of Abraham might come on the Gentiles through Jesus Christ; that we might receive the promise of the Spirit through faith... And*

> *if ye be Christ's, then are ye Abraham's
> seed, and heirs according to the
> promise.* (Galatians 3:14, 29)

As a born again believer, practically every promise made to Abraham or Israel belongs to you. Part of your birthright as a seed of Abraham is the God-given power to acquire wealth. He placed that power within you. You won't offend Him by using it.

Does God really want you to prosper? Look at Psalms 35:27 and see.

> *Let them shout for joy, and be glad, that
> favour my righteous cause: yea, let them
> say continually, Let the Lord be
> magnified,* <u>*which hath pleasure in the
> prosperity of his servant*</u>*.*

According to this verse, watching His servants prosper doesn't give God heartburn, it gives Him pleasure! Think of it. God is pleased when you increase!

This is a theme that is woven throughout the entire Old Testament and continues right on into the New. Look at 2 Corinthians 9:11 for example. Paul says Christians who give to the work of the Gospel are:

Being enriched in every thing to all
bountifulness, which causeth through us
thanksgiving to God.

The NIV translation of this verse is enlightening. It reads, "You will be made rich in every way so that you can be generous on every occasion, and through us your generosity will result in thanksgiving to God."

In that verse and throughout that entire chapter, Paul tells you to expect great financial increase if you are a giver to the work of God. The clear aim of this passage is to raise your level of expectancy concerning your financial harvest. Look at verses 6-8 for example:

But this I say, He which soweth
sparingly shall reap also sparingly; and

*he which soweth bountifully shall reap
also bountifully. Every man according as
he purposeth in his heart, so let him
give; not grudgingly, or of necessity: for
God loveth a cheerful giver. And God is
able to make all grace abound toward
you; that ye, always having all
sufficiency in all things, may abound to
every good work.*

Here is one of the clearest expressions of the will of God for your finances in all of Scripture! When you give cheerfully and abundantly, God wants you to expect Him to bless your finances. Why? So you can squander money on the desires of your flesh? No! So you may continue to "abound to every good work."

The very words of Jesus Himself confirm this biblical truth:

*Give, and it shall be given unto you;
good measure, pressed down, and
shaken together, and running over, shall
men give into your bosom. For with the*

*same measure that ye mete withal it
shall be measured to you again.* (Luke
6:38)

*And Jesus answered and said, Verily I say
unto you, There is no man that hath left
house, or brethren, or sisters, or father, or
mother, or wife, or children, or lands, for
my sake, and the gospel's, But he shall
receive an hundredfold now in this time,
houses, and brethren, and sisters, and
mothers, and children, and lands, with
persecutions; and in the world to come
eternal life.* (Mark 10:29, 30)

It would take volumes to cover all the Bible has
to say about God's desire to see His faithful ones
prospered and successful. Just look at the lives of
the great men of God. Abraham, David, and
Solomon were all blessed with great wealth by
God. We are also His children and heirs
according to the promise. The blessing of God is
meant to be a part of our lives.

STEWARDING HIS RESOURCES

When we talk about giving, there is a key ement that must be understood, and it is the econd lens through which we must view rosperity. It is the most basic call of God on each f our lives—to be God's steward.

Stewardship is the one calling that we all have 1 common: it transcends all dispensations and ollows us into eternity. We are created to manage reation on God's behalf, to manage or dministrate the household or estate of our Lord. he essence of the principle of stewardship is this: ve don't own anything. We are God's stewards, nd we need to see our life as a resource—time, alent, money, etc.—to the accomplishment of od's purpose in the earth.

First Corinthians 4:2 says, "Moreover it is equired in stewards, that a man be found aithful." We see here that a requirement for stewards is that they be found faithful. But how are they to be faithful? Luke 16:10-11 tells us:

He that is faithful in that which is least is faithful also in much: and he that is unjust in the least is unjust also in much. If therefore ye have not been faithful in the unrighteous mammon, who will commit to your trust the true riches?

Here we see that the least that God expects us to be faithful in is our handling of "unrighteous mammon." (The phrase "unrighteous mammon" is a reference to money; however, this is not saying that money is either good or evil. Mammon, or money, only becomes "unrighteous" when it is used wrongly.)

As stewards, we need to be faithful to follow God's commands, particularly in this area of finances. Because faithfulness on any level is impossible until you become faithful in the use of your money. You see, prosperity doesn't involve just your bank account. Prosperity also includes prosperity in your soul, an abundance of health, your every need provided for—body, soul, and spirit. That's why it is vital to understand that giving of our natural resources (money) is the least that we are called to be faithful in. It is intricately entwined with everything else in our life.

Understand, however, that once you learn to be faithful with your money, it doesn't mean you're automatically going to be faithful in all the other areas of your life. There are other steps that must be taken in order to become faithful in those areas. What it does mean is that you simply cannot become faithful in any other area without first taking care of the money matter.

Next, I want to emphasize the latter portion of Luke 16:11. "If therefore ye have not been faithful in the unrighteous mammon, who will commit to your trust the true riches?"

The most important thing I want you to see in this verse is this: if you haven't learned to be faithful with your money, "who will entrust to you the true riches?"

What are the true riches? The true riches are the gifts and callings of God, His power and anointing, and His divine endowments. These are the true riches that God desires for each of us to manage as His stewards on the earth—for the purpose of initiating change on His behalf.

If we don't understand and function in this most basic of all callings, then everything else is superfluous. It won't work right. We are here to manage life and life's resources on behalf of God to fulfill His plan and His purpose. But unless we learn to first become faithful in that which is least—properly stewarding our money—we'll not be entrusted with His true riches. Until we understand and accept this call as God's steward, prosperity can never be born in our life, not by the hand of God.

Chapter Three

GOD'S PURPOSE
FOR PROSPERITY

The third lens that we need to look through to see God's purpose for prosperity is the understanding of how God expects us to earn our money. In Ephesians 4:28 it says, "Let him that stole steal no more. But rather let him labor, working with his hands the thing which is good, that he may have to give to him that needeth."

Some people read this verse casually and assume it to say that if you've been a thief, then get a job and start living right. But Paul is actually giving us his definition of what a thief is. The first thing he says is that if you don't want to be a thief and you don't want to steal anymore, get a job and begin to "labor at that which is good." Dictionaries define that word *labor* as a diligent, consistent effort. This is God's way for you to generate an income. He wants you to be hardworking and persistent in your vocation.

Unfortunately, there are a lot of folks punching the clock in the morning, doing as little as they can during the day, and leaving early in the afternoon. That's not God's way. You give it your most consistent, most diligent effort, and God says if you don't do that, you're a thief. You won't have Him involved in your financial life if you're not making a diligent, consistent effort at that which is good.

In Luke 10:7, Jesus said that the laborer who works diligently is worthy of his hire. Whatever you do, if you do it as though unto the Lord, God will see to it that you get a fair wage.

Ephesians 4:28 also shows us what our motive should be for laboring: "Labor at that which is good that you may have to give to him that needeth." If this isn't your perspective, then he says you're a thief.

I know that's a strong statement. But the reasoning behind it is this. You're God's steward. And when you start laboring for motives that are self-centered, the income that you generate will be consumed on you instead of where He wants t consumed. As God's steward, if you're consuming resources on yourself, He says you're a thief.

God wants our paradigm regarding prosperity to be outward and not inward—to meet the needs of others and not to be consumers on our own flesh. That, my friends, is the purpose of prosperity.

Chapter 4

UNDERSTANDING
THE TITHE

Now that these three lenses are in place, we can begin to properly view how God intends for us to use our money. As I said before, as God's stewards in the earth, the least that He expects us to be faithful in is our money. And being faithful with our money begins with the tithe.

The Tithe Predates the Law

There are those in the body of Christ who argue that the tithe is not in the New Testament and that it was under the law; therefore, Christians are not required to tithe. Both of these assumptions are wrong. The fact is that the tithe predates the Law and it is in the New Testament. To clear up this erroneous doctrine, let's look at a few verses. Look at Hebrews 6:20:

> Where Jesus has entered in for us [in advance], a Forerunner having become

*a High Priest forever after the order (with
the rank) of Melchizedek. (Amp.)*

Jesus' present-day ministry is as our high priest
He is seated at the right hand of God. He is ou
mediator, our advocate, and our intercessor. I
says Jesus was a high priest after the order o
Melchizedek. He was not a high priest after the
order of the Aaronic priesthood, which was unde
the Mosaic Law.

To better understand Jesus' high priestly
ministry, we need to know more abou
Melchizedek. The first mention of Melchizedek is
in Genesis 14:18-20:

*And Melchizedek king of Salem brought
forth bread and wine: and he was the
priest of the most high God. And he
blessed him [Abraham], and said,
Blessed be Abram of the most high God,
possessor of heaven and earth: And
blessed be the most high God, which
hath delivered thine enemies into thy
hand. And he gave him tithes of all.*

Abraham had just been victorious in battle and was returning with the spoils when he met Melchizedek. Upon meeting Melchizedek, Abraham acknowledged him as a priest of the most high God and as such, he paid Melchizedek tithes of the spoil of battle. Abraham tithed before God gave Moses the law! So we see clearly that tithing is not under the law.

Melchizedek in his meeting with Abraham did two things. He received Abraham's tithes and then conferred blessing upon him.

Like Melchizedek, Jesus too receives tithes. Look at Hebrews 7:8:

> *Here mortal men receive tithes, but there he receives them, of whom it is witnessed that he lives.* (NKJ)

Like Abraham acknowledged Melchizedek by paying him the tithe, we too acknowledge Jesus as our high priest by paying Him the tithe. And like Melchizedek blessed Abraham in return, Jesus too confers His blessing on our lives.

Let me ask you this question? How inconsistent is it then to expect His blessing when we have not acknowledged Him as our high priest with our tithes?

The Confession of Our Faith

Now let's look at a verse that tells us how we can further access Jesus' high priestly ministry. Hebrews 3:1 says:

> Therefore, holy brethren, partakers of the heavenly calling, consider the Apostle and High Priest of our confession, Christ Jesus. (NKJ)

Another translation terms it "the confession of our faith." Through this Scripture, we see that we appropriate the benefits of Jesus' ministry through the confession of our faith. We see this same principle again in Hebrews 4:14:

> Seeing then that we have a great High Priest who has passed through the

heavens, Jesus the Son of God, let us
hold fast our confession. (NKJ)

It is our responsibility to hold fast to our confession of faith. And it is Jesus' responsibility to respond to our confession of faith. He can't respond to your confession of faith if you don't have one.

We can apply that principle to us in this way. There are many people who habitually give their tithes to the Lord. Unfortunately, they do it for the wrong reasons. Some feel condemned or shamed into tithing. Some feel that if they didn't tithe, God would be angry with them. Others fear the pastor may change his opinion of them if he knew they didn't tithe.

While they do pay their tithe, they do it for the wrong reason and, consequently, apply no faith to it. They fail to make any confession of faith regarding their tithe; as a result, they do not reap the supernatural blessings from tithing. We must do both. Pay tithes to Jesus, our high priest, with a right heart motive and then make a confession of our faith so He can respond to our faith.

Where Does the Tithe Go?

Does God need your money? No. But it is through the tithe that we acknowledge His sovereignty. God looks at the tithe as our recognition of His lordship and our declaration that we have submitted our interests in this material world to Him. Leviticus 27:30 shows us that God views the tithe as His.

> *And all the tithe of the land, whether of the seed of the land, or of the fruit of the tree, is the Lord's: it is holy unto the Lord.*

The tithe is not something we give God. It's something that we pay Him. How to pay the tithe is a question for many people. Malachi 3:10 gives us the answer:

Bring ye all the tithes into the storehouse, that there may be meat in mine house, and prove me now herewith, saith the Lord of hosts, if I will not open you the windows of heaven, and pour you out a blessing, that there shall not be room enough to receive it.

It clearly states, we're to bring all the tithe to the storehouse. (Notice it does not say, "Divide your tithe up and send it to a number of different storehouses.") What then is the *storehouse*? In the dispensation of the church age, the word *storehouse* is analogous to the local church. In other words, you are to bring your tithe to the local church of which you are a member.

Too often, I hear of people sending off their tithe checks to their favorite traveling ministers. Although they are on the right track in giving to ministries that are doing God's work, they are doing it out of order. First, all the *tithe* (10% of your gross income) goes to your home church. After that, you are free to give *offerings* (monetary gifts above and beyond the tithe) to other ministries.

Malachi 3:10 explains why all the tithe goes to the storehouse: "Bring ye all the tithes into the storehouse [church], that there may be meat in mine house."

The term *meat* here is a reference to natural provision. Meaning, the tithe provides unencumbered general fund income to pay for the cost of ministry.

Also, the word *meat* in the New Testament is a word that is used for the Word of God. (Hebrews 6; 1 Corinthians 3) God is saying that when you bring your tithe to your storehouse, the meat of God's Word will help you grow spiritually. In other words, if you want to receive the meat of the Word of God in your church, you've got to be a tither. The tithe is the first step toward receiving a consistent diet of the meat of God's Word in your life. It's a spiritual exchange.

This spiritual exchange is also illustrated in 1 Corinthians 9:11 where the apostle Paul said, "If we have sown unto you spiritual things, is it a great thing if we shall reap your carnal things?" This verse clearly indicates that there is an exchange of natural for supernatural—an exchange of money for spiritual provision.

Over the years, I've seen this principle in play over and over again. People who never get plugged into church, who never grow spiritually, and eventually disappear altogether are those people who fail to pay God the tithe. But the people who are faithful with the tithe are the ones who get the most blessed and are set apart by God for various responsibilities and calls on their lives.

They learned to be faithful in that which is least, thereby building for themselves a foundation from which they could become faithful in every other area of their lives.

Furthermore, this spiritual exchange is made glaringly clear in the last part of Malachi 3:10 "...prove me now herewith, saith the Lord of hosts, if I will not open you the windows of heaven, and pour you out a blessing, that there shall not be room enough to receive it."

To the tither, God says He will open the windows of heaven and pour out a blessing that there isn't room enough to receive it all. That's quite a supernatural exchange on your giving, wouldn't you say?

But before you start jumping up and down, you need to understand that the phrase "you won't be able to receive it all," is not to be taken as literal. He's not saying you'll have so much money you can't open enough bank accounts to accommodate it all. He is saying that you won't have enough room in your heart to receive all that He's brought you, and the result will be, your heart desires will change. The tithe turns a hard heart into a sowing heart. Why is that? Jesus said in Matthew 6:21, "For where your treasure is, there will your heart be also." When you begin investing your money the way God says as a faithful steward should do, your heart will begin to change.

Now when you talk about God pouring out a blessing, people begin to conjure up in their minds pictures of them winning the lottery,

nheriting a million dollars, or a bag of coins
dropping out of heaven.

(Don't hold your breath on any of that
happening.)

The blessing of God will manifest in your life
through various things like God giving you witty
ideas on how to save or earn extra money. Many
people have the testimony that before tithing they
lived paycheck to paycheck. After they began
tithing, their current income somehow became
more than enough to meet their needs.

Another interesting phenomena that tithers
experience is that the number of financial
emergencies is drastically lowered. They find that
the lawnmower doesn't break down, the car
keeps running smoothly, and the refrigerator
keeps "fridging." Like the children of Israel
wandering through the dessert, they find
(figuratively speaking) that their sandals never
wear out!

For the tither, God opens doors of opportunity
that no man can shut.

Consequences of Not Tithing

Speaking through the prophet Malachi, God said to the Israelites:

> *Even from the days of your fathers ye are gone away from mine ordinances, and have not kept them. … Will a man rob God? Yet ye have robbed me. But ye say, Wherein have we robbed thee? In tithes and offerings. Ye are cursed with a curse: for ye have robbed me, even this whole nation."* (Malachi 3:7-9)

The children of Israel learned that failing to pay the tithe brought a curse upon them and upon the land. Now that's not to say that God will curse you if you don't tithe. What that means is when you do not acknowledge God's supremacy in your life by obeying Him with your money, His "umbrella of protection" is no longer available to you. You are then vulnerable to the enemy's attacks against your life.

(Though the term "umbrella of protection" is not literally in the Bible, the principle very clearly is.)

Finally, I want to call your attention to an important stipulation with regard to tithing. God says "prove me now herewith, saith the Lord of Hosts…" We are to "prove Him" in this.

Some people hear about the tithe and decide that they'll "try tithing for a few weeks and see what happens." No! You don't try tithing. God says that we are to prove Him in this.

How do we prove Him in this? You make a decision to base your life on the Word of God. You make a commitment to tithe simply because God says to. When you make that commitment to Him, then He commits Himself to you and He'll pour you out a blessing there's not room enough to receive!

Meeting the Needs of Your Family

So far, we've learned as God's stewards that the least that we are to be faithful in is the use of our money. We've also learned that we are to generate income by "laboring at that which is good." And from the fruits of our labor, we are to pay God the tithe, which is ten percent of our gross income. And we pay "all" the tithe to "the" storehouse, which is the church we attend.

So then after you've generated an income and given God ten percent, the Bible says in 1 Timothy 5:8 that the next thing you do with your money is to take care of the needs of your family.

> *But if any provide not for his own, and specially for those of his own house, he hath denied the faith, and is worse than an infidel.*

Before we go on a vacation, before we buy a boat, and before we give money to the Gospel we are to meet the needs of our family. If you don't, it's tantamount to being an infidel, an unbeliever.

Meeting the needs of your family is a serious matter to God. It's vital that they have the ecessities in life—food, clothing, and shelter are he barest essentials.

How do we define what a "need" is? In defining vhat need is, there are two things you need to eep in mind. First of all, "need" is a very personal hing. Only you and God know what "needs" our family has. So don't let anybody else define or you what need is for your family. And don't ver get in the business of trying to define omebody else's need.

And your level of need will change with the evel of responsibility God entrusts you with. For xample, a person who is single will have much ewer needs in life than someone who is married ind has children. The level of need rises Irastically once someone becomes married and hen rises again after he or she starts having :hildren.

Secondly, God knows when you've stepped icross the line and try to define something as a leed when it really is a "desire." Don't try to con 3od. He knows the difference between "genuine" need and "false" need. And when you're honest before God about it, He will see to it that you will always have enough left over to meet the need of others.

Do you know what we call money that is "leftover"? We call it seed. Seed is what we use to meet the needs of those around us. And seed is also the instrument God uses to bring increase into your life. So we need to spend some time talking about the seed.

Chapter 5

THE SEED—YOUR INSTRUMENT FOR INCREASE

When we talk about using our leftover money to meet the needs of others, we need to have an understanding of how the needs of others are met. Do we use our excess money to purchase a bag of groceries for someone that can't afford any food? Do you fill up someone's car with gas? Do we slip him a twenty dollar bill when you shake his hand?

Though these are all charitable things to do, they will not, however, meet the greatest need in a person's life. No amount of money can purchase a man's salvation. No amount of money can purchase a healing. The only thing that meets human need on every level consistently and permanently is the Word of God. So consequently, the seed that you have left over is best used to get the Word of God into the hearts of others.

As a matter of fact, in Matthew 13, Jesus defines seed as the Word of God. The soil that the seed is planted in is the human heart. When the seed of God's Word concerning salvation, healing, or deliverance is sown into the hearts of the lost, then the people who sowed the seed are entitled to a 30-, 60-, 100-fold harvest of that seed.

You see, when you give your money to a ministry to help spread the Gospel, you are planting the seed of God's Word into the hearts of those that, that ministry preaches to.

Galatians 6:7 says, "Be not deceived; God is not mocked: for whatsoever a man soweth, that shall he also reap." Your experience of prosperity is based on how effectively you use what is left over to get the Word into other people. Because your harvest in life is not dependent on tithing. It's not dependent on how much you grow and mature in the knowledge of the Word. No. Your harvest in life is dependent upon how you use your life's resource to get the Word of God into other people.

Regretfully, many people make the mistake of "eating" their seed that is left over. There's omething that they've been wanting for a long ime and so instead of planting the seed, they "eat" it. Without knowing it, they've shut off their means of increase and prosperity.

When you make the heart commitment to give your extra seed to "him that needeth," then God will see to it that your desires for these other things will be fulfilled. He'll make a way for you to get them. He loves you and wants to see you increase. But if your heart's desire is to consume that seed instead of give it, then you've blocked Him from bringing those things to you.

Now, I've been referring to your extra "left-over" money as seed. One time Jesus referred to money as seed. But then in the parable of the sower, Jesus referred to the Word of God as seed. So which is it? Is seed money or is it the Word of God?

The only time that Jesus ever referred to money as seed is when it was given to support the preaching of the Gospel.

Otherwise, God would be a respecter of persons. If our harvest in life depends entirely on what a man sows (or how many people he can get to hear the Word), then that would give preachers an unfair advantage. Why? Because most people are not preachers, who have the distinct advantage of speaking to large amounts of people. So instead, we are told in Galatians 6 to use our money to support those that preach or teach the Word. Meaning that when you give money to support the preaching of the Gospel, in a vicarious sense, that is your way of preaching the Word into the lives of the lost. Do you see this? God gives you as much credit for getting the Word to the lost as the person that did the preaching. So this is what Jesus meant when He said to sow our money. Otherwise, seed is normally understood to be the Word of God.

I want to show you a Scripture that illustrates this very point. I'd like us to look at the account of the feeding of the five thousand in John 6:5-7. It says:

*Then Jesus lifted up His eyes, and seeing
a great multitude coming toward Him,
He said to Philip, "Where shall we buy
bread, that these may eat?" But this He
said to test him, for He Himself knew
what He would do. Philip answered
Him, "Two hundred denarii worth of
bread is not sufficient for them, that
every one of them may have a little."*
(NKJ)

Phillip was puzzled by what Jesus said; he clearly didn't get the picture. He was trying to tell Jesus that they didn't have enough money to buy enough bread for everyone to get his fill.

Then Andrew piped up and said, "There is a lad here who has five barley loaves and two small fish..." But then his mind got the best of him too. He said, "...but what are they among so many?" (V 9)

Jesus then said, "Make the people sit down." (V 10) In Mark's account, Jesus had them all sit down in companies and ranks to prepare them to receive a supernatural miracle.

The Bible says that there were five thousand men there. Most Bible commentaries suggest that with women and children present, the total number of people would have probably totaled 20 thousand people.

After everyone was seated, Jesus took the bread and when He had given thanks, He broke it and began to distribute it to the disciples and they, in turn, distributed it to the multitude. He did the same thing with the fish.

Then it says when everyone had their fill, Jesus had the disciples gather up the leftovers. After they gathered everything up, they had a total of 12 baskets of leftovers. Approximately 20 thousand people were fed with five barley loaves and two small fish and they had 12 baskets full of leftovers.

Commentaries say the baskets were most likely woven market baskets, and one of those baskets would have accommodated at least 30 to 50 of the little boy's lunch. And they ended up with 12 baskets full! That's 600 lunches left over after one was sown.

That's a 600-fold return. And just whose return was it? One commentary suggested that there was one basket left over for each disciple. But that's wrong. The disciples didn't sow the lunch. It was the little boy's. Therefore, it was his return.

So what is the lesson learned from this account of the feeding of the five thousand? It's this. The little boy could have given his lunch to someone that seemed to be hungrier than he was. According to the Word, he would have received a 30-, 60-, 100-fold return on his giving. But because he gave it to ministry, 20 thousand people were fed with the little boy's lunch instead of just one.

We see in this example that giving to ministry ordained by God multiplies the effectiveness of the seed sown. And I would suggest as well that it multiplies the magnitude of the harvest returned.

So again, we see the big picture of God's purpose for money.

CONCLUSION

As I said in the beginning, there are many principles found in the Word of God which contribute to your being empowered to prosper. I encourage you to study them as they all work together and none of them can be disregarded.

I have shared with you in this book what is needed for you to lay a solid foundation upon which you can begin winning (God's way) in the financial arena.

I encourage you to allow the Bible to adjust your perspective. God really does want you to prosper as you view life through the stewardship lens and work hard with the motive of having to give to those in need.

It doesn't matter what your background or current financial situation is; if you adjust your perspective, align your actions with the principle of the tithe, and are faithful to sow the seed that God provides, you will be on His pathway to prosperity. Soon, you—a willing and cheerful giver—will literally have become a clearinghouse for the work of God. Hallelujah!

Please note, this article was written from the series *Aligning Our Lives With His Good Pleasure* (for the complete series, see ad on next page).

ABOUT THE AUTHOR

Mac Hammond is host of the nationally distributed half-hour *Winner's Way* broadcast; he has also authored several internationally distributed books including *Positioned for Promotion* and *How to Simplify Your Life.*

Mac Hammond graduated from Virginia Military Institute in 1965 with a Bachelor's degree in English. Upon graduation, he entered the Air Force with a regular officer's commission and reported for pilot training at Moody Air Force Base in Georgia. He received his wings in November 1966, and subsequently served two tours of duty in Southeast Asia, accumulating 198 combat missions.

Between 1970 and 1980, Mac was involved in varying capacities in the general aviation industry including ownership of a successful air cargo business serving the Midwestern United States. A business merger brought the Hammonds to Minneapolis where they ultimately founded Living Word Christian Center in 1980 with 12 people in attendance.

After more than twenty years, that group of twelve people has grown into an active church body of more than 8,500 members. Today some of the outreaches that spring from Living Word include Maranatha Christian Academy, a fully accredited, pre-K through 12th grade Christian school; Maranatha College, an evening and weekend college with an uncompromising Christian enviornment; Living Free Recovery Services, a state licensed outpatient treatment facility for chemical dependency; 3 Degrees, a cutting-edge Christian music club which is smoke/alcohol free; The Compassion Center, a multi-faceted outreach to inner-city residents; CFAITH, an online cooperative missionary outreach of hundreds of national and international organizations providing faith-based content and a nonprofit family-oriented ISP; and a national and international media outreach which includes hundreds of audio/video teaching series, *A Call to Prayer* and the *Winner's Way* broadcasts, the *Prayer Notes* publication, and *Winner's Way* magazine.

The Way of the Winner:
Running the Race to Victory

Angels at Your Service:
Releasing the Power of Heaven's Host

Plugged In and Prospering:
How to Find and Fill Your God-Ordained
Place in the Local Church

Water, Wind & Fire: Understanding the
New Birth and the Baptism of the Holy Spirit

Who God Is Not: Exploding the Myths
About His Nature and His Ways

Winning the World: Becoming the Bold
Soul Winner God Created You to Be

Books by Lynne Hammond

The Master Is Calling: Discovering the
Wonders of Spirit-Led Prayer

Renewed in His Presence: Satisfying Your
Hunger for God

When Healing Doesn't Come Easily

Secrets to Powerful Prayer: Discovering the Languages of the Heart

The Spiritual Enrichment Series (four books by Lynne, recently retitled)

When It's Time for a Miracle: The Hour of Impossible Breakthroughs Is Now!

Staying Faith: How to Stand Until the Answer Arrives

Heaven's Power for the Harvest: Be Part of God's End-Time Spiritual Outpouring

Living in God's Presence: Receive Joy, Peace, and Direction in the Secret Place of Prayer

Dare to Be Free!

The Table of Blessing: Recipes From the Family and Friends of Living Word Christian Center

For more information about this ministry or a complete catalog of teaching tapes and other materials available, visit our website at **mac-hammond.org** *or write:*

Mac Hammond Ministries
P.O. Box 29469
Minneapolis, MN 55429-2946